CROSSWORD PUZZLES

FOR YOUR BACKPACK

JUNIOR

TRIP PAYNE

PUZZLE
WRIGHT
JUNIOR
JUNIOR New York

An Imprint of Sterling Publishing Co., Inc.
1166 Avenue of the Americas
New York, NY 10036

PUZZLEWRIGHT JUNIOR and the distinctive Puzzlewright Junior logo
are trademarks of Sterling Publishing Co., Inc.

© 2019 Trip Payne
Cover © 2019 Sterling Publishing Co., Inc.

ISBN 978-1-4549-3540-7

Distributed in Canada by Sterling Publishing
c/o Canadian Manda Group, 664 Annette Street
Toronto, Ontario M6S 2C8, Canada
Distributed in the United Kingdom by GMC Distribution Services
Castle Place, 166 High Street, Lewes, East Sussex BN7 1XU, England
Distributed in Australia by NewSouth Books,
University of New South Wales, Sydney, NSW 2052, Australia

For information about custom editions, special sales, and premium
and corporate purchases, please contact Sterling Special Sales at
800-805-5489 or specialsales@sterlingpublishing.com.

Manufactured in Canada
Lot #:
2 4 6 8 10 9 7 5 3
12/19

Cover design by Kristin Logsdon

sterlingpublishing.com
puzzlewright.com

CONTENTS

INTRODUCTION

EACH PUZZLE IN THIS BOOKS HAS what's called a "theme": something that the longest answers in the puzzle all have in common. A lot of times, it's clear what the theme is: U.S. presidents, farm animals, or something straightforward like that.

For a lot of puzzles in this book, though, the theme isn't quite as obvious. If you can't figure out immediately what the long answers have in common, take a closer look. It might be that those answers contain words that have something in common. For example, YANKEE DOODLE, CHICKEN NOODLE, and FRENCH POODLE all contain words that rhyme with each other, and SUMMER SCHOOL and WINTER SPORTS both begin with a season of the year.

I hope you have fun figuring out all those answers!

—*Trip Payne*

ACROSS

1 Tools for cleaning up spills on floors
5 Big pigs
9 Spend money
12 Mystical glow
13 Where Cleveland is
14 Tell a falsehood
15 What you're solving right now
17 Museum's collection
18 Note after "fa" on the musical scale
19 "___ and the Tramp" (Disney movie)
21 Perform in a play
24 Charge for a professional service
26 First man in Genesis
29 Let other people know some news: 3 words
33 ___ code (part of a phone number)
34 What a baseball player wears on the head
35 "For ___ a jolly good fellow ..."
36 Person from Kuwait or Iraq, typically
39 Just a little ___ (not much)
41 Sense of humor
43 "Presto!" or "Abracadabra!": 2 words
48 Christmas ___ (December 24)
49 What happens in a movie
50 Black-and-white cookie
51 Place to sleep
52 Complete collections
53 Labor Day's month: Abbreviation

DOWN

1 ___ and cheese (pasta dish)
2 "Let's put ___ heads together"
3 Expert
4 Bratty talk
5 Made sounds like a coyote
6 Exclamation that's similar to "Aha!"
7 Person who grows up to be a woman
8 Soft drink
9 Toy that has its own Fun Factory: Hyphenated
10 What you blow into a balloon
11 Up to this point
16 Couch
20 "See saw, Margery ___ ..." (nursery rhyme)

21 Weak ___ baby:
2 words

22 Lifesaving technique:
Abbreviation

23 Paid the bill for everyone
else

25 "And lots more":
Abbreviation

27 "My lips ___ sealed"

28 Physicians' degrees:
Abbreviation

30 "Let's play it by ___"

31 Things you do all the
time without thinking
about them

32 ___ fail (something that
doesn't work, big-time)

37 Electric guitars are
plugged into them

38 Bundle of cotton or hay

40 Duos

41 What a spider spins

42 "Now ___ seen
everything!"

44 Acquired

45 Valuable stuff that's
found underground

46 Democrat's political
opponent: Abbreviation

47 Small, round mark

ACROSS

1 ___ Sandler (movie comedian)
5 Drink slowly
8 What kids do during recess
12 Something that a dog might gnaw on
13 "I'm ___ loss for words": 2 words
14 Part for an actress
15 Sweet round pastries with a glaze on them: 2 words
18 Belonging to you and me
19 Toy that spins around
20 "Crime does not ___"
22 Cleaning tool that's dipped into a bucket of water
24 Exams
28 Got older
30 Neither this ___ that
32 Mob scene in the streets
33 Secret messages
35 Church bench
37 ___ a finger on (touch)
38 Gorilla, for example
40 Destiny
42 Sweet round pastry with a colorful filling: 2 words

48 Young child's term for a bump or bruise
49 ___ and outs
50 Outbreak on a teenager's face
51 Root ___ (type of soft drink)
52 Pointy item in the grass at a golf course
53 ___ Carrot (fluorescent Crayola crayon color)

DOWN

1 Start of the alphabet
2 "___ have to repeat myself?": 2 words
3 Ticked off
4 List of food options in a restaurant
5 Delilah had his hair cut off, in the Bible
6 "How was ___ know?": 2 words
7 Gasp for air
8 ___ noun (capitalized word like Tennessee or Timothy)
9 "That's hilarious!" in a text message
10 Everything

11 "Sure!"
16 Upper limb
17 Decay
20 ___-Man (classic 1980s video game)
21 Back in the past
23 Burst like a balloon
25 Complete quiet
26 Off ___ good start: 2 words
27 Pigpen
29 Person who gives you cards, in blackjack

31 Say no to
34 Secret agent
36 What a dog's tail can do
39 Make changes to a rough draft
41 "Easier said ___ done"
42 Career
43 Female sheep
44 Be deceitful
45 Six minus five
46 Game with Skip and Reverse cards
47 Dime's value, in cents

3

ACROSS

1 Opposite of north
6 Taylor Swift's type of music
9 Baby goat
12 Bert's roommate on "Sesame Street"
13 "___ we there yet?"
14 Poison ___ (plant that makes you itch)
15 Walked through shallow water
16 "I have to think about this ...": 2 words
18 Outer border
20 Trees with acorns
21 Not him
23 Tall shade tree
25 Two-___ bottle
28 Grains in Cheerios
30 Barbie's boyfriend
32 "My country, 'tis of ___ ..."
33 Go in one ear and out the ___
35 "You're ___ the boss of me!"
37 Santa's little helper
38 Swelled heads
40 Pull behind
42 Daily amounts of medicine
45 From Dublin or Belfast, for example

48 ___-inspiring (stunning)
49 Mopey style of music
50 Weird and spooky
51 "Who Wants to ___ Millionaire": 2 words
52 Get ___ of (toss out)
53 Like the taste of ocean water

DOWN

1 Use a needle and thread
2 "Would you like a cup ___ cone?" (question at an ice cream shop): 2 words
3 A "Little Mermaid" song about living away from land: 3 words
4 Made a knot
5 "Over the ___" (2006 animated movie)
6 Buddy
7 Its slogan is "Milk's favorite cookie"
8 White part of a daisy
9 A "Little Mermaid" song about making a romantic gesture: 3 words
10 "___ never heard of such a thing!"

11 Colorful dip for Easter eggs
17 Short play
19 Large, moose-like animal
21 "Boo-___" (crying sound)
22 Dine
24 Guys
26 "Electric" fish
27 Hockey official, for short
29 Company known for Sonic the Hedgehog
31 Silently indicate "yes"
34 "Who Framed ___ Rabbit" (animated movie)
36 Attempts
39 Prefix for "finals" or "colon"
41 Neighborhood
42 Apply lightly, like makeup
43 Have debts to pay
44 Turf
46 Stop standing
47 "___ Diddle Diddle"

ACROSS

1 Person who has money but hates to spend it

6 Flat ___ pancake: 2 words

9 Disney dwarf who wears glasses

12 "You two need to set ___ your differences"

13 "For what ___ worth ..."

14 Make a mountain out ___ molehill: 2 words

15 Present that's given in December: 2 words

18 Drink in a kettle

19 Insect that makes honey

20 Uncooked

23 Lightweight metal

25 Crunchy Mexican treats

29 Salt Lake City's state

31 Not high

33 Uncommon

34 Took a cut of someone's income

36 Quick swim

38 "Don't ___ stranger!": 2 words

39 Piece of firewood

41 Tiny bite

43 Decoration for a 15-Across: 2 words

50 "___ on Pop" (Dr. Seuss book)

51 New Year's ___ (December 31)

52 Hit the delete button

53 An hour after noon

54 Tree whose name sounds like "you"

55 Did some stitching

DOWN

1 Big ___ (fast-food burger)

2 Ending for "fool" or "child"

3 Polite term of address for a man

4 Revise, as a manuscript

5 Button that starts things over

6 Point an arrow at a target

7 Pierce with a fork

8 Valuable quality

9 "Where ___ start?": 2 words

10 "Don't bite ___ more than you can chew"

11 Cougar or cheetah, for example

16 Where a scorpion's stinger is

17 Shift into high ___ (start moving faster)

20 Same old boring routine
21 "Did I catch you ___ bad time?": 2 words
22 Candle's material
24 ___ off (start to fall asleep)
26 Taxi
27 Portland's state: Abbreviation
28 Where Aquaman lives
30 Assist
32 Bird's "arm"
35 Only one of the Seven Dwarfs without a beard

37 Water flows through them
40 Donate
42 Peel, like apples
43 "___ cares?"
44 Harry and Hermione's friend at Hogwarts
45 Chimpanzee, for one
46 Word that starts the names of four U.S. states
47 Furry foot
48 Suffix for "Japan" or "Vietnam"
49 Fire truck's main color

ACROSS

1 Sack
4 Dish that usually contains lettuce
9 Aladdin's pet monkey in the Disney movie
10 Girl who visits Wonderland
11 City roads: Abbreviation
14 "Ready or ___, here I come!"
15 Casual short-sleeved shirts with collars
16 "Ralph Breaks ___ Internet" (2018 movie)
17 "No ___, no glory" ("You have to be brave")
19 Word that usually goes with "neither"
20 Region
21 Baby on "Family Guy"
23 ___ situation (when there aren't any possible good results): Hyphenated
25 Color of a strawberry
26 Kind of tree that grows from a 7-Down
27 Very, very fat
29 Statement that might end with "... or else!"
32 Device to catch a mouse
33 "I cannot tell a ___"
35 Prescription amount
36 Fish that looks like a snake
37 Carbonated soft drinks
39 "Don't ___ that tone of voice with me!"
40 Early internet service provider
41 Soap ___ (daytime drama series)
42 Playing card between a nine and jack
43 "Beauty and the ___"
44 Pen for piglets

DOWN

1 Hair fringes that cover the forehead
2 "I've got a bad feeling ___ this"
3 Bad result for a bowler: 2 words
4 Maple tree fluid
5 All by yourself
6 "___ & Stitch" (Disney movie)
7 Nut that has a cap
8 ___ Moines (capital of Iowa)

11 Bad results for a batter in baseball

12 At that time

13 Big body of salt water

18 Use a broom

20 Oscar or Emmy, for example

22 Cards that contain personal information: Abbreviation

24 "___-la-la!" ("How fancy!")

27 Popular cookie since 1912

28 Run off to get married

29 Eye drops

30 Desirable quality

31 ___-weeny

32 Drink that may be served hot or iced

34 Original thought

37 Cry out loud

38 Took a chair

6

ACROSS

1 Make brownies or cookies
5 Touch on the shoulder
8 ___ Chang (girl in the Harry Potter books)
11 Not dead
13 Question that sounds like an owl's cry
14 Female chicken
15 Clock or watch, for example
16 Piece of rowing equipment
17 Seeing ___ dog
18 "The First ___" (Christmas song)
20 Lamb's mother
22 Music holders that look like DVDs: Abbreviation
25 Annual payments to clubs
27 Where India and China are
30 What someone clumsy with their hands is said to have
33 ___ loser (bad sport)
34 Bus driver for Bart and Lisa Simpson
35 Mermaid's home
36 Body part that's often pierced
38 Common houseplant

40 Body part with a nail
42 Animal such as King Kong
44 Make fun of
48 Not safe, in baseball
49 "Just you wait and ___!"
50 Strongly dislikes
51 ___ Fields (brand of cookies)
52 A magician might pull a rabbit out of one
53 Payment to a landlord

DOWN

1 Animal that Dracula can turn into
2 "Prince ___" (song in "Aladdin")
3 "___ Possible" (2002–2007 animated series)
4 Tied in score
5 What someone who is clumsy when dancing is said to have: 3 words
6 "I found the answer!"
7 Tiny hole in the skin
8 Swiss, Parmesan, and cheddar
9 "___ Diddle Diddle" (nursery rhyme)
10 Kill two birds with ___ stone

12 Wear away slowly, like a seacoast
19 Currency used in more than 20 countries
21 What a happy dog's tail will do
22 "The Price Is Right" network
23 Two-person group
24 They might be closed to traffic during fairs
26 Place on the internet
28 Its capital is Dublin: Abbreviation
29 Red ___ beet: 2 words

31 Drink that might be "herbal"
32 Upward direction on a map
37 Itchy reaction to poison ivy
39 "So ___ and yet so far"
40 First name of actors Hanks and Cruise
41 "We'll have the time of ___ lives"
43 Split ___ soup
45 Gobbled up
46 One of 100 members of Congress: Abbreviation
47 Suffix that means "most"

ACROSS

1 Fathers
5 "I guess you ___ to be there"
8 Read quickly
12 "This doesn't look good": Hyphenated
13 Redstone, diamond, or iron, in the game Minecraft
14 Group of three musicians
15 Light over a saint's head
16 One plus two plus three plus four
17 Cincinnati baseball team
18 Princess who loved Han Solo, in the "Star Wars" movies
20 Uttered
22 Undergarment that might be lacy
24 Playful bite from a puppy
26 Gets rid of a watermelon seed, maybe
29 What a phone is held next to
30 Garbage
32 "It couldn't have happened ___ nicer guy": 2 words
33 Small, glowing bit of charcoal
35 "___ Willie Winkie" (nursery rhyme)
36 Animal at a dairy farm

37 "American ___" (reality show that Kelly Clarkson once won)
39 Earth's largest continent
41 "___ Want for Christmas Is You" (Mariah Carey song): 2 words
43 "___ a free country!"
45 Sketch
48 Lean to one side
49 Sound made by a 36-Across
50 A razor has a sharp one
51 Very untidy place
52 ___ & Jerry's ice cream
53 "I'd hate to break up ___" ("This collection belongs together"): 2 words

DOWN

1 "Oh, I should have known that!"
2 Cry of surprise
3 Items made of paper that are used to pay for things: 2 words
4 Sneaker or sandal, for example
5 ___ balloon (way to travel in the sky): Hyphenated
6 "Ready when you ___!"
7 Cub Scout groups

8 Single piece of bacon
9 Items made of plastic that are used to pay for things: 2 words
10 First ___ kit
11 Words of refusal
19 Beginning section, for short
21 Remains of a campfire
22 Spelling ___ (word-based competition)
23 Animal associated with the zodiac sign Aries
25 Hamster's foot
27 "This time you've gone ___ far!"
28 Lumber-cutting tool
31 Spring, summer, autumn, or winter
34 Makes modifications to a newspaper article
38 Tree branch
40 Notion
41 Device often found outside a bank: Abbreviation
42 ___ down on the job (slack off)
44 Digit on a foot
46 Number on a birthday cake
47 Moist

ACROSS

1 Sandwich often found in a lunchbox, for short
4 Play-___ (brand of modeling clay)
7 Pet that's wandered off
12 Come ___ screeching halt: 2 words
13 "___ Baba and the Forty Thieves"
14 Got up from one's seat
15 Start of "The Alphabet Song"
16 Color of many roses
17 Bugs that can annoy dogs
18 Male doll in "Toy Story 3"
20 Something to read on a Nook or Kindle
22 Male deer
24 ___ course (entrée)
25 Stubborn ___ mule: 2 words
28 Put on a wall, like a picture
29 Ending for "exist" or "consist"
30 Sharp sound made with the fingers
31 Come to a halt
32 Temporary crazes
33 On the cutting ___ (modern and trendy)
34 Denim pants

36 La Brea ___ pits
37 Groups of two
39 Body part that contains a "drum"
41 Unusual
44 Not yet bright, like a dark lantern
45 It makes you feel self-important
46 "Skip to My ___"
47 North and south ends of the Earth
48 Door unlocker
49 Easy as falling off a ___

DOWN

1 Elementary school support group: Abbreviation
2 Boy's name that reads the same forward and backward
3 They "went up the hill" in a nursery rhyme: 3 words
4 "Rats!"
5 Response to a good bullfighting move
6 Game where people try not to be found: 3 words
7 "Little Miss Muffet ___ a tuffet ...": 2 words

8 Group that's one member smaller than a quartet

9 What Elvis is called "the King of": 3 words

10 "All you had to do was ___"

11 Agreeable answer

19 What a baby chick breaks out of

21 ___ and pieces (various small stuff)

22 "He said, ___ said"

23 Crayola color

24 Spiteful or nasty

26 Get droopy

27 One of Tarzan's jungle friends

30 Deep-___ diving

32 Goes completely without food

35 Great Lake with the shortest name

36 ___ McClure (character on "The Simpsons" who's an actor)

37 Young dog

38 "This is ___-brainer!": 2 words

40 How old you are

42 Scooby-___ (cartoon dog)

43 Used a shovel

ACROSS

1 Opposite of on
4 "This is so amazing!"
7 Beverly ___, California
12 "How funny," in an online chat
13 "Now ___ seen everything!"
14 Disney princess who sings "Part of Your World"
15 ___ the ball (made a mistake)
17 Itty-___
18 The youngest child (with a bird name) in the comic strip "Baby Blues"
19 Balled-up hand
20 "Go ___, make my day!"
22 Popular song
23 Jet ___ (traveler's problem)
26 Hide, like a dog's bone
27 Half a dozen
28 Person who saves the day
29 Food with a yolk
30 Woodpecker's sound
31 Used a toothed tool to cut wood
32 Frosted, like a cake
34 Sounds of Santa's laugh: 2 words

35 The Bloody ___ ("Harry Potter" ghost with a noble title)
37 Chewy ingredient in a Snickers bar
40 Book of maps
41 Vanish into thin ___
42 Gloomy kind of music
43 ___ buds (tongue parts)
44 Attempt
45 Honey ___ Cheerios

DOWN

1 Elderly
2 "Take my word ___ it!"
3 They sprinkle rose petals during weddings: 2 words
4 Cleaned with a towel
5 You cook things in it
6 Tie the knot
7 Bad ___ (repetitive type of behavior you might try to stop)
8 Colored part of an eye
9 Book about Meg, Jo, Beth, and Amy: 2 words
10 Give permission to
11 Crafty

16 Say grace before a meal, for example
19 Repair
20 President Lincoln's nickname
21 Affectionate squeeze
22 Joint just below the waist
24 "Your eyes ___ bigger than your stomach"
25 "___ Bless America"
27 Ready to cry
28 Sound of laughter: 2 words
30 Feeling stressed out

31 Board game where you're trying to get your four pieces into their home space
33 Jacket
34 What Rapunzel let down
35 What a baseball player swings
36 Keep ___ distance: 2 words
37 "The ___ in the Hat"
38 Flightless bird of Australia
39 "You've given me a ___ to think about"

ACROSS

1 Outer edge of a basketball hoop

4 "Let me give this ___ example ...": 2 words

8 Movie

12 "___ disturbing you?": 2 words

13 ___ E. Coyote (Looney Tunes character)

14 Stench

15 Navigation aid on a car's dashboard: Abbreviation

16 Casual shoes a person might wear on the beach: Hyphenated

18 Type of music related to rhythm and blues

20 "Old MacDonald ___ a farm ..."

21 Stand ___ (don't move)

23 Female counterpart of "him"

24 Potato chip container

27 Grip

28 "___ dare you!"

29 Give a darn

30 Hole in a needle

31 Punctuation mark in a Web address

32 "A mind is a terrible thing to ___"

33 Was the champion

34 ___ Place (property in Monopoly)

35 Formal shoes a woman might wear with a dress: 2 words

39 "Plus other things": Abbreviation

42 Dog in "Garfield"

43 Graceful bird with a curved neck

44 "Not a moment ___ soon!"

45 Glass section of a window

46 Campground shelter

47 ___ the table (put out the plates and silverware)

DOWN

1 Cloth used while waxing a car

2 Unruly brat

3 Heat-seeking ___ (kind of long-range weapon)

4 Really horrible

5 Window ledge

6 Muhammad ___ (famous boxer)

7 Son of your sibling

8 What you do to laundry to make it fit in a drawer

9 "What else could ___?": 2 words

10 Chop off, as a dead branch

11 ___ Claus (Santa's wife)
17 Nowhere close
19 "You're a Grand ___ Flag"
21 "___ sells seashells by the seashore" (tongue twister)
22 Yo-yo or Slinky, for example
23 Scalding
24 Containers for Easter eggs
25 School class where you might work with clay
26 "___ whiz!"
28 Truthful
29 Self-driving ___

31 Homer Simpson's annoyed grunt
32 "I ___ talking to you!"
33 Excited cry from a roller coaster rider
34 Figure out what to do ahead of time
35 Move like a frog
36 State whose capital is Boise: Abbreviation
37 ___ rummy (card game)
38 Ram's mate
40 From head to ___ (completely)
41 Foldable bed you might put a sleeping bag on

ACROSS

1 Best bud
4 ___ Vegas, Nevada
7 "___ Dragon" (2016 Disney movie)
12 Country north of Mexico: Abbreviation
13 Point, as a camcorder
14 The mermaid in "The Little Mermaid"
15 Snooze
16 Training ___ (young girl's undergarment)
17 Dangerous
18 Winnie-___-Pooh
20 Evaluate
22 Go bad, like old milk
24 "Just ___ your best"
25 Key that's pressed to indent a paragraph
28 ___ and robbers (kids' game)
29 Kind of animal Donkey Kong is
30 Fairy ___ (type of children's story)
31 Driver's licenses and birth certificates, for example: Abbreviation
32 How a car's speed is measured: Abbreviation
33 Book that goes from Genesis to Revelation
34 Spelling mistake in a newspaper

35 Not in good health
36 "Let me think ___ it"
39 Woman in a convent
41 Tree that's almost the name of a ticklish "Sesame Street" Muppet
44 Cool ___ Doritos
45 Stopping point
46 Boston ___ Party
47 Items on a to-do list
48 "Send help immediately!"
49 Chicago White ___ (baseball team)

DOWN

1 Bit of wordplay
2 Busy ___ beaver: 2 words
3 Devices such as the HP EliteBook and Apple MacBook Pro
4 Clothing tag
5 What fills lungs
6 Devices such as the Samsung Galaxy and Google Pixel
7 Birthday celebration
8 Great Lake that Cleveland is next to
9 "___ the season to be jolly ..."
10 "Oh no, a mouse!"
11 Devious

19 Belonging to that guy
21 "___ you sure about that?"
22 Physics or biology, for example: Abbreviation
23 Pea container
25 Devices such as the Apple iPad and Amazon Fire
26 Opposite of nothing
27 "Honey" or "bumble" bug
29 Mobile download
30 "Open 9 ___ 5" (store sign)
32 Legends from Greece and Rome, for example
33 Ties securely
34 Push in, like a shirttail
36 What Rembrandt and Picasso created
37 Sound from a ram
38 Roll-___ (some deodorants)
40 Card game where you want to play off your high-point cards
42 Summer zodiac sign
43 The Grinch's dog

ACROSS

1 ___ office (place to buy stamps)
5 Place to store valuables
9 Low-___ (like some yogurt)
12 State that's north of Missouri
13 "I could get ___ to this!"
14 Be in debt
15 Shel Silverstein book about a generous plant: 3 words
18 Request
19 Change from brunette to blonde, maybe
20 Speedy plane
22 Ending for "disk" or "Smurf"
25 Snug as a bug in ___: 2 words
29 Became elderly
31 ___ Majesty (queen's title)
32 List of computer options
33 Was dressed in
34 Opposite of west
36 Count ___ Count ("Sesame Street" character)
37 High hit in tennis
39 Rock containing metal
41 H.A. Rey and Margret Rey book about a playful monkey: 2 words

48 Busy ___ beaver: 2 words
49 "Guilty" or "not guilty," in a courtroom
50 Mount Everest's continent
51 Paper or plastic container for groceries
52 Thick, flat piece of concrete
53 Minor bit of damage to a car

DOWN

1 Cherry's center
2 "___-la-la!" ("How fancy!")
3 Thick, comfortable piece of clothing worn in the winter
4 Identifies, as in an Instagram photo
5 Alternative to a minivan: Abbreviation
6 "___ was saying ...": 2 words
7 Parts of a car over the tops of the wheels
8 High-strung
9 "Speak ___ yourself!"
10 Feeling of being impressed

11 Peg that a golfer uses
16 Kyle's younger brother, on "South Park"
17 Group of players on the same side
20 Mouth bone
21 Lack of modesty
23 Taurus, in the zodiac: 2 words
24 Drink that's brewed with boiling water
26 Gear that a driver puts a car in before backing up
27 Spanish word for "one"
28 Squirt ___
30 Place to buy cuts of meat
35 ___ shoes (ballerina's footwear)
38 "Sorry, my mistake!"
40 It might have four lanes
41 Taxi
42 Uncle Sam's country: Abbreviation
43 Cloth used in a car wash
44 Salty body of water
45 Chat for hours
46 ___ rummy (card game)
47 Devour

ACROSS

1 Insect
4 Event where prices are lowered
8 Brand of frozen waffles
12 ___ bad mood (cranky): 2 words
13 Broadway show
14 Wasn't honest
15 Animal that's very similar to a turtle
17 Toboggan, for example
18 Toddler
19 "The Princess and the ___" (fairy tale)
20 Meat-and-vegetables dish
22 Chess is one
25 Furious
28 Invisible stuff all around us
29 Disney movie set in China
30 State where Portland and Salem are: Abbreviation
31 Positive response
32 "You ___ live once!"
33 "I just ___ this was going to happen!"
34 Right this minute
36 "For ___ a Jolly Good Fellow"
37 Actor Sandler or singer Levine
39 Really, really big

44 "Oh, for Pete's ___!"
45 Top cards in the deck
46 Anton ___ ("Ratatouille" food critic)
47 Word that ends a prayer
48 Sister of Meg, Jo, and Amy in "Little Women"
49 What items in compost heaps do

DOWN

1 Little ___ (small amount)
2 Family game with a 108-card deck
3 Small, harmless, slithering reptile: 2 words
4 "X marks the ___"
5 Legendary boxer Muhammad
6 ___ Vegas
7 Place for a pirate's patch
8 "Sorry, my mind was somewhere ___"
9 Slow-moving reptile from Mexico and the southwestern U.S.: 2 words
10 "Aw, shucks"
11 Quirky

16 Haul away, as a broken-down car
19 Something to sign a contract with
20 State out loud
21 It's worn around the neck
22 "Son of a ___!"
23 ___ of a sudden
24 The fifth month
26 Last word of "Twinkle, Twinkle, Little Star"
27 Water droplets on a lawn
29 Take care of an overgrown yard

33 "Junior Genius Guides" author Jennings
35 Bad sign of the future
36 ___ browns (breakfast potatoes)
37 Quick ___ wink: 2 words
38 Barrier in a river
39 Chitchat
40 Frozen water
41 Obtain
42 "Where did ___ wrong?": 2 words
43 Simple, portable bed

ACROSS

1 "Did you hear what I ___?"
5 Up to the task
9 Vehicle in a garage
12 Disney character who sings "Let It Go"
13 Gas in many bright signs
14 "I could really ___ a hug"
15 Superman's other identity: 2 words
17 Get ___ of (throw away)
18 Slimy fish
19 "When the going ___ tough ..."
21 ___ talk (coach's speech)
24 "For sure!"
26 African animal with a horn
29 Rowboat paddles
31 "Help!"
33 Like numbers divisible by two
34 A nightmare is a bad one
36 Word that can go after "punching" or "sleeping"
38 Shepherd's female animal
39 Swirl a spoon around in
41 "I knew it ___ too good to be true"
43 "That ___ nothing to do with anything!"

45 Iron Man's other identity: 2 words
50 Have another birthday
51 "I have ___ honest ...": 2 words
52 Region
53 Move your head to signal "yes"
54 Actor who plays the lead role
55 Message sent between phones

DOWN

1 Bit of a minute: Abbreviation
2 100%
3 "Patience ___ virtue": 2 words
4 "How ___ you!" (offended remark)
5 Joints just above your feet
6 Insect that flies around flowers
7 Opposite of short
8 Go in
9 Loopy kind of writing
10 "Just ___ thought!": 2 words
11 Barn's color, frequently
16 Thing needed to start a car's ignition

20 Jack-in-___-box
21 Like two peas in a ___ (very similar)
22 Body part that produces wax
23 Pushed, like a doorbell
25 Cry hard
27 Never-before-seen
28 Eleven minus ten
30 Rested your feet
32 "The Adventures of Tom ___" (Mark Twain book)
35 Catchers' gloves
37 Liquid in a car's tank

40 Plant part that's usually underground
42 Number cited by a sportscaster, for short
43 "Star Wars" hero ___ Solo
44 A week ___ (seven days back)
46 League with a Slam Dunk Contest: Abbreviation
47 "___ you sure about that?"
48 "Toy Story" dinosaur
49 Kit ___ (candy bar)

ACROSS

1 Part of the face where gloss is applied
4 Home for college students
8 Birds that eat mice
12 "Now I understand!"
13 Square footage
14 Strap held by someone riding on horseback
15 Fast food restaurant where you might order Nachos Supreme: 2 words
17 Girl's name that reads the same forward and backward
18 Adam and Eve's garden
19 Sounds that often follow "tra" in a song: 2 words
21 Golden retriever in the Pixar movie "Up"
22 "The ___ Bitsy Spider"
24 Puts down, like carpeting
26 Achy
27 Shows on TV
28 ___ fish sandwich
29 Captain Hook's first mate
30 Tiny little lie
31 Insect stage after larva
33 Dozes briefly
37 Criminals don't obey them

39 Fast food restaurant where you might order a Meat Lover's pie: 2 words
41 Go ___ great length (talk a lot): 2 words
42 "You're the only ___ trust": 2 words
43 Stuff that's excavated from mines
44 Picks up the check
45 Home for baby birds
46 "Nope" opposite

DOWN

1 Not on time
2 "If ___ my way ...": 2 words
3 Walk nervously back and forth
4 Small amount of hair gel
5 End of some nasty threats: 2 words
6 Type of race where a baton is passed
7 Large shopping center
8 "Are you a good witch ___ bad witch?" (question in "The Wizard of Oz"): 2 words
9 Fast food restaurant where you might order a Jr. Bacon Cheeseburger

Grid (across top): cells numbered 1, 2, 3, ■, 4, 5, 6, 7, ■, 8, 9, 10, 11
12, 13, 14
15, 16, 17
18, 19, 20, 21
22, 23, 24, 25
26, 27
28, 29
30, 31, 32, 33, 34, 35, 36
37, 38, 39, 40
41, 42, 43
44, 45, 46

10 Charlie Brown's friend who waits for the Great Pumpkin on Halloween

11 Get caught, like a piece of fabric on a nail

16 Vegetable that's sometimes sliced into rings and fried

20 "I cannot tell ___": 2 words

23 Snare

25 Building for a basketball game

26 Fast food restaurant where you might order a Veggie Delite sandwich

27 Astonishes

28 Princess in "The Princess and the Frog"

29 Backbone

30 Flip-___ (casual sort of shoe)

32 "Once ___ a time ..."

34 Chips ___! (cookie brand)

35 Like 24-karat gold

36 Take a single move forward

38 Roads and avenues: Abbreviation

40 Pimple

ACROSS

1 ___-Man (video game hero who chomps dots)

4 Sacred oath

7 "___ disturb" (sign on a hotel door): 2 words

12 "It wasn't too long ___ that ..."

13 Adam's wife

14 Soap ___ (daytime drama series)

15 Part of the same family

17 Where the Tennage Mutant Ninja Turtles live

18 "When you wish ___ a star ..."

19 "Too ___ cooks spoil the broth"

20 Arrive

22 Cheesy joke

23 Gobble up

26 Tiny dollop of paint

27 Exact duplicate of a plant or animal

29 ___ Baba

30 Letters between R and V

31 Dimly ___ (somewhat dark)

32 Dogwood or redwood, for example

33 Call a halt to

35 "Look ___ talking!"

37 Soft drinks

39 Sound that accompanies lightning

42 Make ___ for oneself (become well-known): 2 words

43 Fish that might be "electric"

44 Proud ___ peacock: 2 words

45 Oscar ___ (brand of bologna)

46 "I'm so frightened!"

47 Until this time

DOWN

1 It's often 2 or 3 for a hole of miniature golf

2 What tree rings indicate

3 When people remember an explorer to America: 2 words

4 Presidential power to kill a bill

5 Where cookies cook

6 Join in marriage

7 How much medicine you're supposed to take at one time

8 Unwrap

9 When people celebrate December changing to January: 3 words

10 State that's north of California: Abbreviation

The grid contains numbered cells: 1, 2, 3, 4, 5, 6, 7, 8, 9, 10, 11, 12, 13, 14, 15, 16, 17, 18, 19, 20, 21, 22, 23, 24, 25, 26, 27, 28, 29, 30, 31, 32, 33, 34, 35, 36, 37, 38, 39, 40, 41, 42, 43, 44, 45, 46, 47.

11 Sticky black goo
16 Animal that beats its chest
19 End of lots of superheroes' names
20 Round items in a music library: Abbreviation
21 Cracklin' ___ Bran (breakfast cereal)
22 "You have ___ to be kidding me!"
24 Ginger ___
25 Formal neckwear
27 Not further away
28 It's right below a mustache

32 Hefty weight
34 Gentle, like animals in a petting zoo
35 Exclamation from a kid on a waterslide
36 Member of the Avengers who turns green
37 Yosemite ___ (cartoon character)
38 Carry ___ conversation: 2 words
39 Golfer's prop
40 Ending for "Milan" or "Taiwan"
41 Cheese-eating rodent

ACROSS

1 What postal carriers carry
5 "For what ___ worth ..."
8 ___-tac-toe
11 Everyone ___ (all the other people)
12 Body of water that sounds like a letter of the alphabet
13 Up there in years
14 Natural attraction on the border of the U.S. and Canada: 2 words
17 Health resort
18 Seeing ___ dog
19 Black symbol of Halloween
22 What a face card is worth in blackjack
24 Outer borders
28 Software buyer
30 "Ha ha ha!," in a text
32 "Hey, that hurts!"
33 It can be used to make a simple ghost costume
35 "It couldn't have happened ___ nicer guy": 2 words
37 "___ Story 4" (Pixar movie)
38 "Send help immediately!"
40 Program on a smartphone

42 Natural attraction on the border of China and Nepal: 2 words
48 Bird that can turn its head almost the whole way around
49 In ___ of (quite impressed by)
50 Pie-baking appliance
51 Wager
52 "You're right!"
53 Encounter

DOWN

1 Adult males
2 Aladdin's alter ego as a prince
3 "My mind ___ blank": 2 words
4 Lower limbs
5 Country whose capital is Jerusalem
6 Alternative to coffee
7 Not in danger
8 Large city in Ohio
9 Needing a doctor's attention
10 Recordings that could be "ripped" or "burned": Abbreviation
15 Quite fitting
16 "Yes," to a sea captain

19 Yellow vehicle used for a class field trip

20 Grime at the bottom of a barbecue

21 Casual shirt for warm weather

23 "You're ___ the boss of me!"

25 Protruding belly

26 Prefix for "system" or "logical"

27 Like an introvert

29 Final outcome

31 Units of bread

34 2,000-pound measure

36 Orangutan or gorilla, for example

39 "Don't move" command to a dog

41 Dance for high-schoolers

42 Angry crowd

43 "I ___ you an explanation"

44 Her mate is a ram

45 Sleek, white robot in "Wall-E"

46 Get a peek at

47 Explosive stuff: Abbreviation

ACROSS

1 "... all ___ are created equal"

4 Major network that isn't NBC, ABC, or Fox

7 Plays a movie role

11 Chopping tool with a sharp blade

12 Ooh and ___

13 Where "an old woman lived," according to the nursery rhyme: 2 words

14 Do some quilting

15 Once ___ blue moon (rarely): 2 words

16 Color of snow

17 Check the fit of, at a clothing store: 2 words

19 Person who's not a newcomer at something

21 Casual hat with a visor

22 Pack away

23 A&W root ___ (brand of soft drink)

24 Former vice president Gore and actor Pacino, for two

25 Genuine

27 Sick as ___: 2 words

29 Wood that's used to make buckets

31 Elmer ___ (cartoon character)

33 It beats scissors but loses to paper

36 Limb that's attached to a shoulder

37 Drink that's usually caffeinated

38 Butter ___ (ice cream flavor)

39 Words a teacher might write on a student's paper if they need to talk: 2 words

41 Material similar to asphalt

43 Game where you don't want a Wild Draw 4 card played on you

44 Prefix with "section" or "national"

45 Pride in oneself

46 ___ and arrow (archery equipment)

47 Scout's merit badge holder

48 Piece of turf

49 One of 100 politicians in the U.S. Capitol: Abbreviation

DOWN

1 Poles that support ships' sails

2 Put forth, like strength or power

3 National League baseball team: 3 words

4 Adam and Eve's oldest child

5 Forbid the use of

6 Circle or oval, for example

7 Black stuff that comes out of a volcano

8 National League baseball team: 2 words

9 Completely wreck

10 Oozes

13 "Don't say ___!" ("Hush!"): 2 words

18 Have debts to pay

20 Spend time with a book

23 Color mixed with red to make purple

26 Opposite of before

28 What miners dig up

29 Watering hole in a desert

30 Big sports stadium

32 Romantic evenings on the town

34 Boat that's similar to a kayak

35 "I should have ___ better"

38 Give a strong nudge to

40 Casual way to say "whatever"

42 Long ___ (in the distant past)

ACROSS

1 Not present or future
5 Really, really big
9 Tried not to be found
12 Get caught in ___ (be revealed to be dishonest): 2 words
13 Apple device that plays songs
14 Vow in a chapel: 2 words
15 Pepsi-___
16 Male companion for a doe
17 Church benches
19 Rhinoceros feature
21 Spanish cheer
22 Central American nation with a canal
24 Read electronically
26 Skateboarder's hands-free leap (and also a boy's nickname)
27 Building brick used in clay homes
30 Stinky scent
32 Mammal that's in the same family as otters and skunks
33 American spy group: Abbreviation
35 "Now ___ getting somewhere!"

37 Musical piece for one person
38 Boy in the "Toy Story" films
40 Bundle of hay
42 Not modern
43 "___ what you did there": 2 words
44 Website addresses: Abbreviation
45 Hair coloring
46 Approves with a head gesture
47 Trickle very slowly

DOWN

1 Ms. ___-Man (classic video game)
2 "Welcome to Hawaii!"
3 Grain storage building
4 Water on sad people's faces
5 ___ and hers
6 Planning something naughty: 4 words
7 Hockey score
8 Boundary line
9 "Hungry Hungry" animal in a kids' game
10 Totally perfect

		1	2	3	4		5	6	7	8
9	10	11		12			13			
14				15			16			
17		18		19		20		21		
22			23		24		25			
26						27		28	29	
	30			31		32				
33	34		35		36		37			
38		39		40		41		42		
43				44			45			
46				47						

11 Took from the internet and put on one's computer

18 Remarked

20 Group that oversees university sports, like March Madness basketball: Abbreviation

23 Cat's comment

25 Tallies up

28 Body part with a "button"

29 Wear away slowly, like a seacoast

31 Picture puzzle

32 "Beauty and the Beast" heroine

33 Abel's brother, in the Bible

34 Not ___ many words: 2 words

36 Uncommon

39 "Sure!"

41 Psychics claim to have it: Abbreviation

ACROSS

1 Goose ___ (things you might get on your skin when it's chilly)

6 "___ we now our gay apparel" ("Deck the Halls" lyric)

9 Keebler cookie maker, in commercials

12 Baseball player from Houston

13 New Year's ___ (December 31)

14 Dairy farm sound

15 House that Luna Lovegood was in, in the "Harry Potter" books

17 Dog breed with a face resembling a bulldog

18 Scoring goal in golf

19 "Some things are better ___ unsaid"

21 Fruity topping for toast

24 Worn, tattered cloth

26 Worker's boost in pay

29 Verbal

31 ___ the Builder (cartoon character)

33 Person who might be undergoing puberty

34 Parents pass them down, and they determine things like eye color and height

36 "How did I miss that?!"

38 Ruby's color

39 Campbell's product

41 ___ off (start to fall asleep)

43 Hula dancer's necklace

45 House that Draco Malfoy was in, in the "Harry Potter" books

50 "Many years ___ ..."

51 Garden tool with a flat blade

52 Black or green topping for a pizza

53 Wasn't the loser

54 "___ about time!"

55 One-___ (not showing all viewpoints)

DOWN

1 Word that can go after "candy" or "space"

2 Country that declared its independence in 1776: Abbreviation

3 Network that was originally known for airing pop stars' videos

4 ___ school (private school before college)

5 Detection device in a submarine

6 Pop singer Lana ___ Rey

7 Not-quite-circular shape

8 More up-to-date

9 Less full

10 "Skip to My ___"

11 Heavy haze

16 Kind of animal Sebastian is in "The Little Mermaid"

20 Opposite of skinny

21 Pace between "walk" and "run"

22 "Where ___ you going?"

23 Rich person's very large house

25 "In ___ we trust" (phrase on U.S. currency)

27 Catch sight of

28 Put a halt to

30 Zodiac sign before Virgo

32 Hit a short ground ball, in baseball

35 Japanese raw fish dish

37 Chocolate snack cakes made by Hostess: 2 words

40 Hatch a scheme

42 Place to buy ham or roast beef

43 ___-abiding citizen

44 An arrogant person has a big one

46 "I agree with you"

47 Get ___ of (throw away)

48 "___ got work to do"

49 Homer's goody-goody neighbor on "The Simpsons"

ACROSS

1 ___ and flows (moves like the tide)
5 Close friend
8 Container for okra or peas
11 Pop-___ (brand of breakfast pastries)
13 Boxer Muhammad who was played in a movie by Will Smith
14 What people getting married say: 2 words
15 Sound you might hear when walking in a haunted house
16 "___ be the judge of that!"
17 Round holders of software or music: Abbreviation
18 Disney character who makes a deal with Ursula
20 "Let me ___ you a question ..."
22 Liquid in a pen
24 ___-mo replay
25 Say "1, 2, 3, ..."
28 "The early bird ___ the worm"
30 Fast food chain with Bucket Meals
32 NBA player from San Antonio
33 Go in one ear and out the ___

35 "I didn't know which ___ to turn"
37 Muddy pen on a farm
38 Female in a flock
39 Miles ___ (not anywhere close)
41 "___ like to tell people ...": 2 words
43 Have a ___ to pick (complain about something minor)
45 Brand of marshmallow chicks and bunnies
48 ___ Tac (brand of breath mints)
49 Ending for "Vietnam" or "Japan"
50 Extra tire in a car trunk
51 Tool that resembles a hatchet
52 What soldiers fight in
53 "Peter Pan" pirate

DOWN

1 Abbreviation after a list of things
2 Salad ___ (feature of many restaurants)
3 Start a conversation among quiet people: 3 words
4 Light in the night sky
5 What Jack and Jill went up the hill to fetch: 3 words

6 The whole enchilada
7 Light purple flower
8 Begin to go faster: 3 words
9 Not even, in math
10 List of ___ and don'ts
12 Equipment needed for some winter sports
19 Large, moose-like animal
21 Letters that mean "Emergency!"
22 "Where did ___ wrong?": 2 words
23 Badminton court divider
26 What a bolt fits into

27 Have a taste of
29 Do some needlework
31 Soft hat
34 Sign up for another year's subscription
36 Sounds from small dogs
40 Weight training units
41 ___ standstill (not moving): 2 words
42 Number of points scored for a touchdown, in football
44 "This ___ recording": 2 words
46 ___-K (young kid's school)
47 Visualize

ACROSS

1 "___ you sure about that?"
4 Bed in a soldier's tent
7 Gently move in the breeze
11 Football player from Los Angeles
12 What goes through a snorkel
13 Nevada or Nebraska, for example
14 Half of four
15 Common winter virus
16 What people pay to the IRS
17 Reason for overtime, in sports
19 "Don't count your chickens before ___ hatch"
21 "You could hear ___ drop": 2 words
23 Cry of delight at an amusement park
24 Glide on snow
27 Eventually: 3 words
30 Baby chick's mother
31 Geeky person
32 Place where money is kept
33 Curve in a road
34 ___ talk (coach's speech)

35 Tool for sweeping
38 "A long time ___ in a galaxy far, far away ..."
40 Judge's field
43 Sooner than required
44 Went faster than jogging
45 Private ___ (detective)
46 Changed hair color
47 Breakfast food that might be scrambled
48 Stoplight's color

DOWN

1 What museums display
2 Not cooked at all
3 Jealousy, anger, or joy
4 Small restaurant
5 Liquid that food is fried in
6 Game where you tell secrets and do risky things: 3 words
7 "Don't go yet"
8 Dental floss coating
9 Dined on
10 "Definitely!"
13 Man of ___ (Superman's nickname)

18 No room at the ___
(problem for Mary and
Joseph in the Bible)
20 Bunch of cattle
21 Pikachu's owner, in
"Pokémon"
22 "Star Wars" pilot ___
Dameron
23 Little brown songbird
24 Office tool for
connecting papers
25 Doll who worked for
Lotso in "Toy Story 3"

26 Get on the nerves of
28 The Joker, to Batman
29 President Lincoln's
nickname
33 Fearless
34 Ping-___ (table tennis)
35 Place for a nap
36 Beam of light
37 Mined metallic
mineral
39 Prank
41 "All in favor" vote
42 Become spouses

ACROSS

1 Household animals
5 Type of tree often bought at Christmas
8 "That's what they ___ say"
11 Medical checkup
12 "How old ___ you?"
13 Mediterranean ___ (large body of water)
14 Breakfast cereal that goes "snap, crackle, pop": 2 words
17 Shoe bottom
18 Get a look at
19 Animal that flies in a cave
21 Lower limb
23 ___ the truth (doesn't lie)
27 Thing on a list
29 Mouse ___ (computer accessory)
31 ___ before you leap
32 It comes before tomorrow
34 "Don't ___ words in my mouth"
36 French word for 37-Across
37 Opposite of no
39 Treasure hunters follow them

41 Chocolatey breakfast cereal: 2 words
46 Hot dog ___ stick: 2 words
47 Floor covering that's soft
48 40-day period before Easter
49 Rain-soaked
50 ___-cone (frosty treat)
51 ___-Bake Oven (toy)

DOWN

1 Limit one ___ customer
2 Lived
3 Crispy Mexican snack
4 Use your nose
5 ___ away (distant)
6 Eye part that might be blue or brown
7 Button that starts things over
8 "___ was saying ...": 2 words
9 Sara ___ (brand of frozen desserts)
10 ___ Vegas, Nevada
15 Hang on to
16 Banana's covering
19 ___ part (actor's small role)

20 From ___ Z (including everything): 2 words
22 Narrow opening
24 Makes less tight, like a necktie
25 Cindy ___ Who (young girl encountered by the Grinch)
26 Compete in a slalom
28 White sandwich spread, for short
30 Unintelligent
33 365- or 366-day periods

35 Piece of furniture in a dining room
38 Whirled around
40 "Guilty" or "not guilty," to a judge
41 Animal with an udder
42 "If there's ___ thing I know for sure ..."
43 Animal that meows
44 Vain person's problem
45 Pen where you'd hear oinking

ACROSS

1 Sound from a ram or ewe
4 Something fun to play with
7 Plots
12 Expensive black liquid
13 "___ things a little differently": 2 words
14 Consume completely: 2 words
15 Undergarment similar to a bikini top
16 State that borders Texas, Arkansas, and Mississippi
18 Root ___ (kind of beverage)
20 ___ and reel (fishing gear)
21 Talks to God
23 "Mayday!"
24 "Who am ___ judge?": 2 words
27 Capital of Italy
28 Grown-up boy
29 "I ___ it all along"
30 "Now just hold ___ minute!": 2 words
31 Animal that's a source of steak
32 ___ wave (destructive surge of water)
33 "Oh! I see it now!"
34 "Where ___ go wrong?": 2 words

35 State that borders Minnesota, Iowa, Illinois, and Michigan
39 "That's a tough ___ to follow!"
42 Is sore
43 Insect in a hill
44 Word typically used with "neither"
45 Birds whose young are called goslings
46 "Signs point to ___" (Magic 8 Ball response)
47 Win at ___ cost

DOWN

1 ___ for apples (take part in a Halloween activity)
2 ___ conditioner (cooling device used in the summer)
3 State that borders Tennessee, Georgia, Florida, and Mississippi
4 Scrabble pieces
5 Strong scent
6 "Pleased to meet ___"
7 Mexican coins
8 ___-back (relaxed)
9 Arrive ___ decision: 2 words
10 Female counterpart of a monk

11 Hot tub
17 ___ Man (one of the Avengers)
19 Bull's-___ (center of a dartboard)
21 Expert
22 Second-youngest Weasley child, in the Harry Potter books
23 Cutting tool
24 State that borders Michigan, Ohio, Kentucky, and Illinois
25 Beverage associated with England

26 Bird that's thought to be wise
28 ___ and groan
29 Young goat
31 Selected
32 Shades of color
33 What ones are called in Yahtzee
34 Have a fine meal
35 Puppies' tails do it
36 Frozen water
37 That girl
38 Put into words
40 Prisoner, in slang
41 Put forth some effort

25

ACROSS

1 Attorney's profession
4 Do something
7 Alternative to a burrito
11 Cold, transparent cubes
12 Find a spot for a car
14 "He's ___ of his word" ("You can trust him"): 2 words
15 Kitchen tools for figuring out amounts of ingredients: 2 words
18 Dull person
19 Animals like Bambi
20 Have in one's view
21 Extra charges
23 "Who lives in a pineapple under the ___?" ("SpongeBob SquarePants" question)
24 Suffix that means "most"
25 "___ your thinking cap on!"
27 Drink very slowly
29 Tap lightly on the head
32 That girl
34 Gestures of approval
37 "To ___ is human; to forgive, divine" (saying that means "It's okay to make mistakes")

38 Body parts that hula dancers shake
40 Online destination
42 Kitchen tools for making shapes in dough: 2 words
45 Paintballs and BBs, for example
46 Thrown ___ loop: 2 words
47 Generation ___ (difference between two age groups)
48 Dozes briefly
49 ___-speed bike
50 Possess

DOWN

1 Arm or leg
2 ___ spades (specific example of a 5-Down): 2 words
3 "Here ___!" (what people say when they arrive somewhere): 2 words
4 Hindu character on "The Simpsons"
5 One of 52 items in a deck
6 Attempts
7 Tic-___-toe (simple game)
8 Cause to laugh

9 Bullfighters wave them in front of bulls
10 Beginning phase
13 Leg joints
16 Ooze through the cracks
17 Wheat or rice, for example
22 Japanese raw fish dish
26 Burglar
28 ___-it note
29 Butter ___ (ice cream flavor)
30 Pleasant smell

31 Walk heavily
33 Walt Disney World theme park
35 San ___ Padres (baseball team)
36 Scarecrow stuffing
39 "You bet!"
41 Channel that announces sports results
43 Decisive blows, in boxing: Abbreviation
44 Light brown

ACROSS

1 Stopped living
5 Swimmer in an aquarium
9 It shows you the way to your destination
12 Notion
13 Stumble ___ (find by accident)
14 "I could really ___ a hug"
15 What "re" is a drop of, in the song "Do-Re-Mi": 2 words
17 Word that can follow "buzz" or "hack"
18 Disappointed
19 2008 Disney movie about a TV-star dog
21 Chatter
24 Pull behind a truck
26 Posteriors
29 Spinning like ___: 2 words
31 Distant
33 Group of three
34 He has a sleigh led by reindeer
36 ___-tickling (very funny)
38 "___ we now our gay apparel" ("Deck the Halls" lyric)
39 True statement
41 Chicken ___ (childhood disease)
43 ___ lodge (winter resort)
45 Vacation for a newly married couple
50 "Along came a spider who sat down beside ___"
51 Where Adam and Eve originally lived
52 Breakout on many teenagers' faces
53 Part of a needle that's threaded
54 Female pigs
55 Figure on the back of a baseball card, for short

DOWN

1 Use a spade
2 "What else could ___?": 2 words
3 Sea creature that the Grinch is compared to, in a song
4 Male parents
5 Feeling warmly toward: 2 words
6 Drive-___ (outdoor movie theaters)
7 The part of a concert ticket you keep
8 Maid of ___ (person in a wedding ceremony)
9 Yellow covering for a hot dog
10 Quick ___ wink: 2 words
11 Place to sit in church
16 Have a sandwich, maybe

1	2	3	4		5	6	7	8		9	10	11
12					13					14		
15				16						17		
			18				19		20			
21	22	23		24		25		26			27	28
29			30		31		32		33			
34				35		36		37		38		
		39			40		41		42			
43	44			45		46				47	48	49
50				51					52			
53				54					55			

20 "___ It Go" ("Frozen" song)
21 Car fuel
22 ___ later date (in the future): 2 words
23 Type of blaze you might see at an evening beach party
25 The Civil ___
27 ___ de Janeiro, Brazil
28 Bart Simpson, to Homer Simpson
30 Group that raises funds for schools: Abbreviation
32 Becomes ready to harvest

35 Pains
37 Young fellow
40 Phrase at the top of an errand list: 2 words
42 December 25 holiday, for short
43 Pronoun for a woman
44 White or black part of a piano
46 ___ and improved
47 When Columbus Day occurs: Abbreviation
48 "___ scale from 1 to 10 ...": 2 words
49 Back part of a soccer goal

ACROSS

1 Becomes less bright
5 Wrestling cushion
8 Water in a SuperSoaker, for short
12 Egg-shaped
13 "Would you like a cup ___ cone?" (question at an ice cream shop): 2 words
14 St. ___, Minnesota
15 "Dr. Jekyll and Mr. ___"
16 Mornings: Abbreviation
17 Boundary line
18 "I know exactly what you ___"
20 It might be true-false or multiple-choice
22 College houses for men, for short
24 Evil curse
25 Place for a hearing aid
28 Floor covering
29 "___ my case!": 2 words
31 Ginger ___ (bubbly beverage)
32 Carry ___ conversation: 2 words
33 Smog pollutes it
34 Speedy
36 Metal found in pennies
38 In ___ land (spaced out): Hyphenated
39 Be patient

41 ___-haw (donkey's sound)
43 ___ and crafts
46 "___ of Green Gables"
47 Food with a yolk
48 Friend of Kyle and Cartman on "South Park"
49 Part of a flower below the petals
50 Kanga's son in "Winnie-the-Pooh"
51 Spelling mistake an editor finds

DOWN

1 Homer Simpson's cry
2 ___ League (group of eight colleges)
3 Humor publication whose mascot is Alfred E. Neuman: 2 words
4 Frozen rain
5 Sound made by someone in pain
6 What a sweater sleeve covers
7 Has a little sample of some food
8 Hairy animals in a jungle
9 Event attended by Alice and the March Hare: 3 words

10 Container for hot chocolate, maybe
11 Spanish cheer
19 From Japan or the Philippines, perhaps
21 Member of the crowd, on a film set
22 Walk to and ___
23 Go fast on foot
24 Not him
26 Name of the prince that Aladdin pretended to be
27 Color of Superman's cape

30 Wealthier
35 Only as ___ resort: 2 words
37 Single object
38 "The ___ Batman Movie"
39 Past tense of "is"
40 Bug you might see on a kitchen counter
42 "I'm the greatest" feeling
44 Noisy style of dancing
45 ___-Caps (brand of chocolate candy)

ACROSS

1 Frosty the Snowman had a corncob one
5 "___ and the Tramp" (Disney movie)
9 "American ___" (TV talent show)
10 Unit of farmland
11 Highest part
14 Ill
15 "You're putting me ___ awkward position": 2 words
16 Anton ___ ("Ratatouille" food critic)
17 Just fine, in astronaut lingo: Hyphenated
18 Increased in size
19 Comic-Con attendee, for example
20 Tattles
22 Rocks
24 Fasten, like shoelaces
25 "Is it ___ wonder?"
26 Failed to strike the target
29 Large group of people
31 Solo for an opera singer
32 "It would mean ___ to me if ...": 2 words
34 Dine

36 Jon's girlfriend in the comic strip "Garfield"
37 "Don't lose sleep ___ it"
38 List of what the chef can make
39 Ending for "Peking" or "Siam"
40 Three times three
41 ___ in a while (occasionally)
42 Finds the sum of
43 They're covered by a blindfold

DOWN

1 Leaning Tower of ___ (Italian landmark)
2 Dummy
3 Very small: Hyphenated
4 Large, moose-like animal
5 Dens for wild animals
6 Pimply skin condition
7 Makes a picture with a pencil
8 Japanese money
11 Very small: Hyphenated
12 Creature like Shrek

13 Peas come in them
18 ___ club (singing group)
19 Something you should never do: Hyphenated
21 Girl who plays the saxophone on "The Simpsons"
23 Miniature fruit pie
26 Masculine
27 Type of flower, or a part of the eye

28 He defeated Goliath in the Bible
29 Uneaten parts of apples
30 Rumba or samba, for example
33 ___ a hand (help out)
35 Day after Monday: Abbreviation
37 Go ___ diet: 2 words
38 "Eeny, meeny, miney, ___"

ACROSS

1 Sombrero, for one
4 ___-leaf clover (lucky find)
8 What you get when you put two numbers together
11 Belly muscles
12 A matter of ___ and death
13 iPhone download
14 Many underwater swimmers, all together: 3 words
17 ___-bitsy (very small)
18 "___ be right back"
19 Golfers' vehicles
21 Cunning
22 Stand ___ (don't take new cards)
25 "What am I getting myself ___?"
26 Note between "fa" and "la"
27 Tennis ___ (sneaker)
28 Commercial messages
29 Early parts of the day: Abbreviation
30 Weighing device in the bathroom
31 Marriage vow words: 2 words
32 Pass across a bar code reader

33 Many cows and bulls, all together: 3 words
38 Some time ___ (back in the past)
39 Shed a ___ (cry a little)
40 Tool used in a rowboat
41 Boy's name that is a word meaning "show agreement" backwards
42 In this very place
43 Physicians: Abbreviation

DOWN

1 "This ___ never happened before!"
2 Alphabet's first letters
3 Casual tops: Hyphenated
4 Dental string
5 Covered in grease
6 Alien's ship, to earthlings: Abbreviation
7 What you might get in a restaurant when your glass is empty
8 Travel by boat
9 Fruit Roll-___ (chewy snacks)
10 55 ___ (common speed limit): Abbreviation
15 Sergeant Snorkel's dog in the comic strip "Beetle Bailey"
16 Bug you might swat

19 American spy group: Abbreviation
20 What "&" means
21 Letters that mean "Emergency!"
22 "Star Wars: Episode I – The ___ Menace"
23 Internet service provider that made its debut in 1991
24 Golfer's prop
26 Not rough
27 "Beat it, kitty!"
29 Put in, like a recipe ingredient
30 Terrify
31 Wrinkle-removing appliance
32 Mufasa's brother, in "The Lion King"
33 "Old MacDonald ___ a farm ..."
34 Sense of personal pride
35 Banking charge
36 Lard ___ Donuts (snack shop on "The Simpsons")
37 Busy hospital areas: Abbreviation

ACROSS

1 Container for pickles
4 The good ___ days
7 Underneath
12 "Ice ___" (animated movie)
13 Drink that's popular in Japan
14 ___ Ingalls Wilder (author of "Little House on the Prairie")
15 Female parent
16 Beef patty on a bun
18 Not shut
20 Money used in Tokyo
21 Nile or Mississippi, for example
23 "___ a free country!"
24 Jumbo ___ (large airplane)
27 Kitchen appliance that gets hot
28 Card that is sometimes high and sometimes low
29 Sister of Meg, Jo, and Amy in "Little Women"
30 Where sheets and pillows are found
31 "I'll ___ anything once"
32 11-Down's opposite
33 Name of the toucan mascot of Froot Loops
34 Back of the foot
35 Chopped-up beef in sauce, on a bun: 2 words

39 Fluid that flows in pipelines
42 Creepy, like a haunted house
43 "That's what they ___ say"
44 Card game where you might play a blue 8
45 Layers of paint
46 "You bet!"
47 Used a sofa

DOWN

1 Spread you might have with peanut butter
2 "It wasn't too long ___ that ..."
3 Took away
4 "On the ___ hand ..."
5 Low-fat, like meat
6 Barrier in a river
7 Rhythm and ___ (type of music)
8 ___ a living (make money)
9 Carry with great effort
10 What redstone is in the game Minecraft
11 Major international conflict
17 Small unit of memory for a computer

19 Item that might use ink refills
21 Take illegally
22 "Oops, ___ said too much!"
23 Covered with frost
24 Full of envy
25 And many more: Abbreviation
26 Word that begins many movie titles
28 Largest branch of the U.S. military
29 Insect that makes a buzzing sound

31 Cassettes
32 Takes the skin off a fruit
33 "___ it out!" ("Say it already!")
34 Target in miniature golf
35 Sixtieth of a minute: Abbreviation
36 Lion of the zodiac
37 "Is it a boy ___ girl?": 2 words
38 Blue bird
40 Needle ___ haystack: 2 words
41 Place for parking at a mall

ACROSS

1 What a baby might call its mother
5 Get ready to throw a dart
8 Small argument
12 Resident of Iraq or Jordan, typically
13 Biology, for one: Abbreviation
14 Jafar's parrot, in "Aladdin"
15 Cincinnati's Major League Baseball team
16 Small, in many rappers' names
17 Created a portrait
18 Body part that contains a drum
19 Strawberries have them on the outside
21 Countryside hotel
22 Person who looks after kids when their parents are out
24 Amount to be paid
26 Leaky faucet's sound
27 Fifty percent
28 A ___ "apple": 2 words
29 People who dig for gold, for example
31 Stuff to dunk chips in
32 Baked ___ (things like cakes and pies)

34 One of the four highest cards in a deck
36 "What more can ___?": 2 words
38 Man of the family
39 What a blizzard consists of
40 "That's ___!" ("Not true!"): 2 words
41 Last number in a countdown
42 Rancher's unit of land
43 Clear part of a telescope
44 Moved fast
45 Casual summertime shirts

DOWN

1 Female horse
2 Locations
3 European capital where you could see bullfighting: 2 words
4 "Six-pack" muscles
5 Not awake
6 More likely to cause you to slip, as a wintertime road
7 Opposite of spicy, in terms of salsa
8 Kid who lives next door to Andy, in "Toy Story"

Grid numbering: 1 2 3 4 | 5 6 7 | 8 9 10 11 (row 1), 12 | 13 | 14 (row 2), 15 | 16 | 17 (row 3), 18 | 19 | 20 | 21 (row 4), 22 23 | 24 25 (row 5), 26 | 27 (row 6), 28 | 29 | 30 (row 7), 31 | 32 33 | 34 35 (row 8), 36 | 37 | 38 | 39 (row 9), 40 | 41 | 42 (row 10), 43 | 44 | 45 (row 11)

9 European capital where you'd find the Eiffel Tower: 2 words

10 Real estate ___ (house seller)

11 Small city

19 Bee's attack

20 Reads quickly

23 Prefix meaning "three"

25 Cry from a fan to a bullfighter

27 Like the eggs in an Easter egg hunt

28 Passageway between airplane seats

29 Disney movie with the song "How Far I'll Go"

30 Make a basket or a touchdown

31 Face of a watch

33 Body ___ (personal stench)

35 Female animals that bleat

37 ___-or-no question

39 Used a park bench

32

ACROSS

1 Bug that's attracted to a flame
5 The "2" in "1 + 1 = 2"
8 Place with a steam room
11 Coin used in France and Spain
12 Too much ___ good thing: 2 words
13 "I've ___ enough of this!"
14 Film based on toys that can change from cars into other things
17 Box for a model builder
18 "Look, I did it!": Hyphenated
19 Offers a challenge to
22 Word that can go before "gloss" or "balm"
23 Republican's opponent: Abbreviation
26 ___ tea (cool drink)
27 Female bird on a farm
28 Bring up the ___ (be in last place)
29 Group for schoolkids' families: Abbreviation
30 What to cook chili in
31 Party throwers
32 Friendly conversation
34 Baby grizzly bear

35 Film based on toys that can stick together to build things: 3 words
40 Slippery as an ___
41 Near to the ground
42 2,000-pound weights
43 "It just doesn't ___ up" ("This makes no sense")
44 Signal from a sinking ship
45 Make a trade

DOWN

1 Encountered
2 "The odds are not on ___ side"
3 ___-la-la (song sounds)
4 Tooted a car horn
5 Opposite of hard
6 Unexplained light moving in the sky: Abbreviation
7 ___ Prince (nerdy student on "The Simpsons")
8 Place to store gardening equipment
9 Events with floats and marching bands
10 Website pop-ups

1	2	3	4		5	6	7		8	9	10	
11					12				13			
14				15				16				
			17				18					
19	20	21				22			23	24	25	
26					27			28				
29				30				31				
		32	33				34					
	35				36				37	38	39	
	40				41				42			
	43				44				45			

15 Female sibling, for short
16 Treasure ___ (item that might say "X marks the spot")
19 Quick swim
20 Portray a character
21 Arrived at
22 "___ the games begin!"
24 Be a gourmet
25 ___ Fields (brand of cookies)
27 Red buildings in Monopoly

28 Mechanical beings
30 Pen ___ (friend who writes letters)
31 How to play a kazoo
33 Had in one's hands
34 Sources of milk
35 Brown beverage
36 Slimy stuff
37 Formal promise
38 "___ manner of speaking": 2 words
39 Supposed psychic power: Abbreviation

ACROSS

1 Start of "The Alphabet Song"
4 Rock gently
8 Channel for many sporting events
12 Fabric coloring
13 Lois ___ (woman in Superman comics)
14 Blue shade associated with water
15 They fix your teeth
17 Step of a ladder
18 Tank ___ (sleeveless shirt)
19 "Never ___ million years!": 2 words
20 Put on some weight
22 Homer's son on "The Simpsons"
25 Fictional sleeper ___ Van Winkle
28 Where a flu shot is usually injected
29 First sign of the zodiac
30 All Hallows' ___ (October 31)
31 "Golly ___!"
32 Item made by Hallmark
33 Word that ends a prayer
34 Score where neither team is ahead
36 "___ Baba and the Forty Thieves"
37 Garden in the Bible

39 American luxury car maker
44 Go up in flames
45 "They don't make them like they ___ to"
46 ___-surf (search for yourself online)
47 Person in charge of employees
48 Pots and ___
49 "You reap what you ___"

DOWN

1 "Just ___ water" (phrase on powdered drink mix)
2 "Ta-ta!"
3 Small units of length
4 Lose footing on a wet floor
5 "I ___ just about to say the same thing!"
6 White ___ (term for a termite)
7 Opposite of "no"
8 Make money
9 Large units of area: 2 words
10 Bit of wordplay
11 Horse that's past its prime
16 "This must weigh a ___!"
19 "___ not up to me"

1	2	3	■	4	5	6	7	■	8	9	10	11
12			■	13				■	14			
15			16					■	17			
■	18				■			19				■
20	21			■	22	23	24		■	25	26	27
28			■	29				■	30			
31			■	32				■	33			
■	34	35			■	■	36			■	■	■
37	38			■	39	40	41				42	43
44				■	45			■	46			
47				■	48			■	49			

20 Corny joke
21 "Where the Wild Things ___" (Maurice Sendak book)
22 Garment under a blouse
23 Beach ball filler
24 Ketchup color
26 "___ never been so embarrassed!"
27 Ballpoint, for example
29 Playing card that often beats a king
33 The whole ball of wax
35 Small hotels

36 Hearing ___ (devices that assist the hearing impaired)
37 Shrink back from the shore, like the tide
38 The Dynamic ___ (Batman and Robin)
39 Stanley ___ (NHL trophy)
40 Stubborn ___ mule: 2 words
41 Comfortable room
42 A week ___ (seven days back)
43 Calf's mother

34

ACROSS

1 Checkers or dominoes, for example
5 Sudden notion to do something
9 "Well, ___ be darned!"
12 Became elderly
13 Give a ranking to
14 Common gift on Father's Day
15 "We haven't been together in forever!": 4 words
18 Chow down
19 What hogs wallow in
20 Part of the face covered by a beard
23 Valuable stone
25 ___-powered (energized by the sun)
29 Take ___ of (drink slowly): 2 words
31 Nicki Minaj's type of music
33 Speed competition
34 ___ sign (symbol used in subtraction)
36 Metal opener on a soda can
38 "Five Little Monkeys Jumping on the ___"
39 Went faster than just walking
41 Macadamia, for one
43 Pleasantly brief: 3 words

50 "___ could you do such a thing?"
51 Continent with nearly 50 countries
52 Parrot in Disney's "Aladdin"
53 Long, snaky fish
54 Snoozes on the couch, maybe
55 Expand

DOWN

1 Cowboy's term for a woman
2 Many moons ___ (way back when)
3 Sign on one of two restroom doors
4 "I'm on the ___ of my seat!"
5 Author
6 Pink-colored meat
7 Collector's ___ (valuable object)
8 Lists of food and drink at restaurants
9 ___ a Small World (Disneyland ride)
10 Untrue statement
11 First name that can be for either a boy or a girl
16 Word that can follow "price" or "name"
17 Noticeable smell

The crossword grid:

1	2	3	4	■	5	6	7	8	■	9	10	11
12				■	13				■	14		
15				16					17			
■		18				■	19			■	■	■
20	21	22	■	23		24	■	25		26	27	28
29			30	■	31		32	■	33			
34			35	■	36		37	■	38			
■		39		40	■	41		42	■	■	■	■
43	44	45			■	46			■	47	48	49
50			■	51			■	52				
53			■	54			■	55				

20 Traffic ___ (problem for drivers)

21 "Do ___ say!": 2 words

22 Cross the finish line first

24 Cushion for a gymnast

26 Chemistry workplace

27 Playing card with an A in the corner

28 Tomato-colored

30 Kitty's happy sound

32 Chinese animals that eat bamboo

35 Another name for the Devil

37 Passenger vehicle with a long aisle

40 Agency that used to launch space shuttles: Abbreviation

42 Very small tree branch

43 That lady

44 Gardening tool with a long handle

45 Harry Potter's pet named Hedwig, for example

46 Little bite

47 Play it by ___ (wing it)

48 ___ boost (something that increases a person's self-esteem)

49 Roadside rescue

ACROSS

1 Get up on the wrong ___ of the bed
5 $20 bill dispensers: Abbreviation
9 "Knock it ___!"
12 Prayer's conclusion
13 Make small talk
14 Legendary boxer Muhammad ___
15 Was in a chorus
16 ___ fish sandwich
17 Grade that a high school sophomore is in
19 Carpenter's cutter
21 Prefix for "fortune" or "pronounce"
22 Candy Crush ___ (popular game app)
23 Sonic the Hedgehog's game company
24 Scrooge's grumpy shout before "Humbug!" in "A Christmas Carol"
25 First name of Kyle, Stan, and Kenny's friend on "South Park"
27 Entrance's opposite
29 Score to try for on a golf course
31 Storage building in a garden
33 Computer input

36 One of Santa's workers
37 "What she doesn't know won't hurt ___"
38 Academy Award
39 Clump of dirt
41 Sound of discomfort
43 "___ Possible" (TV cartoon)
44 Stick ___ in the water: 2 words
45 Boundary line
46 Full of trickery
47 Agrees without speaking
48 Envisions

DOWN

1 Pageant contestant's diagonal belt
2 "___ little teapot, short and stout ...": 2 words
3 Thickly packed
4 In a relationship headed toward marriage
5 "You need to clean up your ___!"
6 They can attach papers to bulletin boards
7 Crazed feeling
8 Hide away
9 Grains fed to horses

10 ___ and tick collar (something a dog wears)

11 Stuff you eat with your hands: 2 words

18 Black road goo

20 It's used to coat a surfboard

23 Devious plans

26 Suffix for "sheep" or "boy"

28 Cards that contain personal information: Abbreviation

29 Nut often used in pies

30 "I owe it ___ you": 2 words

32 Gradually get worn down, like rocks in a river

34 Dangling part of a kite

35 Group of troops

38 Bills that can be changed for a five

40 ___ Moines (Iowa's capital)

42 How many years you've been alive

36

ACROSS

1 Places for pet canaries
6 Where you might visit a monkey house
9 Big ___ (main tent at a circus)
12 Not dead
13 You might open one on your phone or tablet
14 Feeling that makes you go "Wow!"
15 Bird that's very similar to a crow
16 Miles ___ gallon
17 Male doll that first came out in 1961
18 Halts
20 Jack or Jill, for example
22 Do a downhill run on snow
24 Have a good cry
26 Opposite of sad
29 Under ___ (sworn to tell the truth)
31 "Hump day": Abbreviation
33 Where a bird builds a nest
34 Rough guesses
36 Two, in Spanish
38 "___ only money"
39 "Let's get this show on the ___!"

41 African country that's also a boy's name
43 Tool for hacking weeds
45 "Button your ___!" ("Be quiet!")
47 Giant body of water
50 Shut-___ (people who stay at home)
51 Highest card in a royal flush
52 African animal with a horn
53 "Have we ___ before?" ("Do I know you?")
54 What makes grass slick in the morning
55 Campers sleep in them

DOWN

1 Automobile
2 ___ mode (served with ice cream): 2 words
3 "Stop talking about that already!": 4 words
4 Like all numbers that end in 4
5 Puts in the mail
6 Sound of an electric shock
7 "___ wide!" (dentist's command)
8 Talk show host Winfrey

Crossword grid with numbered cells: 1, 2, 3, 4, 5, 6, 7, 8, 9, 10, 11, 12, 13, 14, 15, 16, 17, 18, 19, 20, 21, 22, 23, 24, 25, 26, 27, 28, 29, 30, 31, 32, 33, 34, 35, 36, 37, 38, 39, 40, 41, 42, 43, 44, 45, 46, 47, 48, 49, 50, 51, 52, 53, 54, 55

9 Be very self-satisfied with: 3 words

10 "You ___ it to yourself ..."

11 Felt-tip ___

19 Mama pig

21 Bathroom rug

22 "Rescue us!"

23 Kit ___ (candy bar)

25 A comforter covers it

27 Animal with a human family

28 "Sure!"

30 Premium cable channel that shows movies

32 "What's up, ___?" (Bugs Bunny's catchphrase)

35 Meat-free meal, sometimes

37 Not long

40 You use five to play Yahtzee

42 Soreness

43 That guy

44 "Just ___ more thing ..."

46 Bench that faces the pastor

48 Insect that's eaten by an aardvark

49 Words of rejection

ACROSS

1 "Just ___ water"
4 "For ___ a Jolly Good Fellow"
7 Oregano or mint, for example
11 Bring a court case against
12 Sturdy wood
13 "I cannot tell ___": 2 words
14 Father of Bart, Lisa, and Maggie: 2 words
17 "___ of Green Gables"
18 Tarzan's hairy friend
19 Breezes are gentle ones
21 "The ___ is falling!" (Chicken Little's warning)
22 Baby bear
25 Chances that something will happen
26 Scheduled to arrive
27 Part of Supergirl's uniform
28 Negative replies
29 Fifty divided by five
30 Small handbag
31 "Just you wait and ___!"
32 Small French restaurant
33 Father of Chris, Meg, and Stewie: 2 words

38 ___-steven (exactly equal)
39 It's pumped into a space suit
40 Most of it is south of Canada: Abbreviation
41 Current events
42 Pellets in kids' toy weapons
43 Internet connection slowness

DOWN

1 Grime at the bottom of a fireplace
2 Musical group that consists of two people
3 Insists on
4 Antlers
5 "Let me put your mind at ___ ..."
6 ___ jumping (Winter Olympics event)
7 Cheerful
8 "What ___ is there to say?"
9 ___ Grande (river on the southern border of Texas)
10 ___ & Jerry's ice cream
15 Completes

16 Construct
19 Took the blue ribbon
20 "___ not like green eggs and ham": 2 words
21 Nearest star to Earth
22 Cautious
23 ___ and downs
24 Nectar-gathering insect
26 Like a ___ in the headlights (stunned)
27 Part of a shirt where you'd use a "link"

29 People aged between 12 and 20
30 Groups of two
31 Thicker-than-soup meal in a bowl
32 Enclosure for a sleeping baby
33 Writing implement that's used to create calligraphy
34 She lived in Eden
35 Talk endlessly
36 "Patience ___ virtue": 2 words
37 Old horse

38

ACROSS

1 "Nope": Hyphenated
5 "Be quiet!"
9 Mountain ___ (soft drink)
12 Location
13 Continent connected to Europe
14 Moody style of rock music
15 Type of place you can live in
17 Nickname for James
18 Loafer, for example
19 Great ___ (large dog breed)
20 Fix stories for publication
24 Microwave ___
25 Type of place you can live in
29 Sticky stuff used in gift-wrapping
30 Mexican food that's folded
31 "Haven't ___ you somewhere before?": 2 words
32 43,560 square feet
36 Lion's ___ (dangerous place)
37 Type of place you can live in

42 "___ you coming or not?"
43 O-shaped treat that begins with O
44 Heidi's mountain range
45 Young Scottish boy
46 Require
47 Glass part of a microscope

DOWN

1 Main Street, ___ (Disneyland section)
2 Body parts that can swivel
3 State with a large Mormon population
4 Person who defeats the villain
5 Meat from a pig
6 Put to good ___ (take advantage of)
7 Subject of a sermon, frequently
8 Item of clothing that's a token in Monopoly
9 "This seems familiar" feeling: 2 words
10 Rapper whose real name is Marshall Mathers
11 "Little ___" (classic Louisa May Alcott novel)

16 ___ off (very annoyed)
19 "___ make myself
   clear?": 2 words
21 Speck
22 "Trust me, ___ doctor":
   2 words
23 ___-tac-toe
25 Something to take a
   selfie with
26 Removed the lid from
27 Item in the middle of a
   badminton court
28 Biblical ark builder

29 ___ wave (destructive
   ocean force)
33 What Santa gives
   naughty children,
   supposedly
34 Regulation
35 Network for fans of
   athletics
37 Unit of weight for whales
38 Raw rock
39 Very small
40 Wordless agreement
41 Suffix for "host" or "lion"

ACROSS

1 Religious women living in a convent

5 Muscles strengthened by sit-ups

8 Bouncing ___ the walls

11 "Come to think ___ ...": 2 words

12 Have a look

13 Child of Kanga in "Winnie-the-Pooh"

14 Mascot of Frosted Flakes: 3 words

17 ___ Baba

18 Relaxing vacation place

19 Neither rhyme ___ reason

22 Snow queen in "Frozen"

25 Put ___ act (pretend): 2 words

28 Comply with

30 Number of years in a decade

31 Eat in style

32 The Flintstones' pet snorkasaurus

33 Droops down

35 Simple bed used by a camper

36 "Which came first, the chicken or the ___?"

38 Fishing pole

40 "The Wizard of Oz" character who sings "If I Were King of the Forest": 2 words

46 Astonishment

47 What "r" might mean in a text

48 Red spots on a teen's face

49 Place to snooze

50 "Talk to you later"

51 Skinny plant in a marsh

DOWN

1 "Failure is ___ an option"

2 Mysterious craft in the sky: Abbreviation

3 ___, Pinta, and Santa Maria (Columbus's ships)

4 Out of ___ (no longer fashionable)

5 First name of Pikachu's owner

6 Scripps National Spelling ___

7 Adjusts, as a clock

8 Grown naturally without added chemicals

9 Lex Luthor, to Superman

10 Making up ___ lost time

15 Leans to one side

16 Apple's mobile music player
19 Agree silently
20 ___-Wan Kenobi ("Star Wars" character)
21 Extended a subscription
23 Where Aquaman lives
24 Mad
26 Pitch ___-hitter: 2 words
27 It's used in volleyball and tennis
29 Relaxing exercise discipline
34 Type of energy or eclipse
37 Quickly take hold of
39 Cubes used to play many board games
40 Car that might be yellow
41 Have loans
42 Moisture-free
43 Sara ___ (brand of frozen pies)
44 "Don't put all your eggs in ___ basket"
45 Nancy Drew's boyfriend

ACROSS

1 Destroy

5 Garfield and Sylvester, for example

9 Gift of ___ (ability to talk easily)

12 "Do ___ others ..." (the Golden Rule)

13 Where Vietnam is

14 Number of players needed to play solitaire

15 Charlie Brown's cry of frustration: 2 words

17 Unexpected

18 Liquid from a maple tree

19 Button that will deliver an email

21 Soft, spongy ground

24 Pay-___-view

26 Wall-E is one

29 Easy as falling off ___: 2 words

31 Pick up the ___ (pay the bill)

33 Suffix for "soft," "flat," or "silver"

34 Love a lot

36 ___ Puff (SpongeBob's boating teacher)

38 "If I ___ the Circus" (Dr. Seuss book)

39 Pick a card

41 Note from a borrower

43 Science classroom

45 Someone who doesn't get upset when they lose: 2 words

50 Covered with frost

51 "To make a ___ story short ..."

52 Popular cookie since 1912

53 Thing that supports a golf ball

54 "When all ___ fails, read the directions"

55 "Better luck ___ time"

DOWN

1 Throw ___ (small floor covering)

2 Colorful card game whose name you have to say when you have only one card left

3 "How was ___ know?": 2 words

4 Shows agreement with a head gesture

5 What Aladdin flew around on

6 "___ always say ...": 2 words

7 Makes a knot

8 Less dangerous

9 Mr. ___ (candy containing peanuts)

10 "Beauty ___ the Beast"

11 Piece of furniture used mainly at night
16 Space between two front teeth
20 Not later
21 Lamb's sound
22 Like grandparents, in terms of age
23 "Farewell!"
25 Los Angeles NFL player
27 "Are you a man ___ mouse?": 2 words
28 Number of amendments in the Bill of Rights
30 Angry dog's snarl

32 The Golden Gate ___
35 Bird on the back of a dollar bill
37 Sailor's call for help
40 Winter sweater material
42 "Stop ganging ___ me!": 2 words
43 Dimly ___ (kind of dark)
44 Blackjack card that can be worth 11
46 Iron-___ (some decals)
47 Mined material
48 T. ___ (type of dinosaur, for short)
49 Preschooler

ANSWERS

1

```
MOPS  HOGS   PAY
AURA  OHIO   LIE
CROSSWORD    ART
   SOL  LADY
ACT  FEE   ADAM
SPREADTHEWORD
AREA  CAP   HES
   ARAB  BIT
WIT  MAGICWORD
EVE  PLOT   OREO
BED  SETS   SEPT
```

2

```
ADAM  SIP   PLAY
BONE  ATA   ROLE
CINNAMONROLLS
   OURS  TOP
PAY  MOP   TESTS
AGED  NOR   RIOT
CODES  PEW   LAY
   APE  FATE
JELLYDOUGHNUT
OWIE  INS   ACNE
BEER  TEE   NEON
```

3

```
SOUTH   POP   KID
ERNIE   ARE   IVY
WADED   LETSSEE
   EDGE  OAKS
HER  ELM   LITER
OATS  KEN   THEE
OTHER  NOT   ELF
   EGOS  DRAG
DOSAGES   IRISH
AWE  EMO   EERIE
BEA  RID   SALTY
```

4

```
MISER   ASA   DOC
ASIDE   ITS   OFA
CHRISTMASGIFT
   TEA  BEE
RAW  TIN   TACOS
UTAH  LOW   RARE
TAXED  DIP   BEA
   LOG  NIP
WRAPPINGPAPER
HOP  EVE   ERASE
ONE  YEW   SEWED
```

5

```
BAG  SALAD
ABU  ALICE   STS
NOT  POLOS   THE
GUTS  NOR   AREA
STEWIE   NOWIN
   RED   OAK
   OBESE  THREAT
TRAP  LIE   DOSE
EEL  SODAS   USE
AOL  OPERA   TEN
   BEAST   STY
```

6

```
BAKE   TAP   CHO
ALIVE  WHO   HEN
TIMER  OAR   EYE
   NOEL  EWE
CDS  DUES   ASIA
BUTTERFINGERS
SORE  OTTO   SEA
   EAR  FERN
TOE  APE   TEASE
OUT  SEE   HATES
MRS  HAT   RENT
```

7

```
DADS   HAD   SCAN
UHOH   ORE   TRIO
HALO   TEN   REDS
  LEIA    SAID
BRA   NIP   SPITS
EAR   TRASH   TOA
EMBER  WEE   COW
  IDOL    ASIA
ALLI   ITS   DRAW
TILT   MOO   EDGE
MESS   BEN   ASET
```

8

```
PBJ   DOH   STRAY
TOA   ALI   AROSE
ABC   RED   TICKS
   KEN   EBOOK
STAG   MAIN   ASA
HANG   ENT   SNAP
END   FADS   EDGE
   JEANS   TAR
PAIRS   EAR   ODD
UNLIT   EGO   LOU
POLES   KEY   LOG
```

9

```
OFF   WOW   HILLS
LOL   IVE   ARIEL
DROPPED   BITTY
   WREN   FIST
AHEAD   HIT   LAG
BURY   SIX   HERO
EGG   TAP   SAWED
   ICED   HOHO
BARON   CARAMEL
ATLAS   AIR   EMO
TASTE   TRY   NUT
```

10

```
RIM   ASAN   FILM
AMI   WILE   ODOR
GPS   FLIPFLOPS
   SOUL   HAD
STILL   HER   BAG
HOLD   HOW   CARE
EYE   DOT   WASTE
   WON   PARK
HIGHHEELS   ETC
ODIE   SWAN   TOO
PANE   TENT   SET
```

11

```
PAL   LAS   PETES
USA   AIM   ARIEL
NAP   BRA   RISKY
   THE   RATE
SPOIL   TRY   TAB
COPS   APE   TALE
IDS   MPH   BIBLE
   TYPO   ILL
ABOUT   NUN   ELM
RANCH   END   TEA
TASKS   SOS   SOX
```

12

```
POST   SAFE   FAT
IOWA   USED   OWE
THEGIVINGTREE
   ASK   DYE
JET   ETTE   ARUG
AGED   HER   MENU
WORE   EAST   VON
   LOB   ORE
CURIOUSGEORGE
ASA   PLEA   ASIA
BAG   SLAB   DENT
```

13

```
BUG   SALE   EGGO
INA   PLAY   LIED
TORTOISE     SLED
   TOT    PEA
STEW  GAME   MAD
AIR   MULAN  ORE
YES   ONLY   KNEW
   NOW    HES
ADAM  GIGANTIC
SAKE  ACES   EGO
AMEN  BETH   ROT
```

14

```
SAID  ABLE   CAR
ELSA  NEON   USE
CLARKKENT    RID
   EEL    GETS
PEP   YES    RHINO
OARS  SOS    EVEN
DREAM BAG    EWE
   STIR    WAS
HAS   TONYSTARK
AGE   TOBE   AREA
NOD   STAR   TEXT
```

15

```
LIP   DORM   OWLS
AHA   AREA   REIN
TACOBELL     ANNA
EDEN  LALA   DUG
   ITSY   LAYS
   SORE   AIRS
   TUNA   SMEE
FIB   PUPA   NAPS
LAWS  PIZZAHUT
ONAT  ONEI   ORE
PAYS  NEST   YEP
```

16

```
PAC   VOW    DONOT
AGO   EVE    OPERA
RELATED      SEWER
   UPON   MANY
COME  GAG    EAT
DAB   CLONE  ALI
STU   LIT    TREE
   STOP   WHOS
SODAS THUNDER
ANAME EEL    ASA
MAYER EEK    YET
```

17

```
MAIL  ITS    TIC
ELSE  SEA    OLD
NIAGARAFALLS
   SPA    EYE
BAT   TEN    EDGES
USER  LOL    OUCH
SHEET TOA    TOY
   SOS    APP
MOUNTEVEREST
OWL   AWE    OVEN
BET   YES    MEET
```

18

```
MEN   CBS    ACTS
AXE   AAH    ASHOE
SEW   INA    WHITE
TRYON PRO    CAP
STOW  BEER   ALS
   REAL   ADOG
OAK   FUDD   ROCK
ARM   TEA    PECAN
SEEME TAR    UNO
INTER EGO    BOW
SASH  SOD    SEN
```

19

```
    P A S T     H U G E
H I D   A L I E   I P O D
I D O   C O L A   S T A G
P E W S   H O R N   O L E
P A N A M A   S C A N
O L L I E       A D O B E
    O D O R   B A D G E R
C I A   W E R E   S O L O
A N D Y   B A L E   O L D
I S E E   U R L S   D Y E
N O D S     S E E P
```

20

```
B U M P S   D O N     E L F
A S T R O   E V E     M O O
R A V E N C L A W   P U G
      P A R   L E F T
J A M   R A G   R A I S E
O R A L   B O B   T E E N
G E N E S   D U H   R E D
    S O U P   N O D
L E I   S L Y T H E R I N
A G O   H O E   O L I V E
W O N   I T S   S I D E D
```

21

```
E B B S   P A L   P O D
T A R T S   A L I   I D O
C R E A K   I L L   C D S
    A R I E L   A S K
I N K   S L O   C O U N T
G E T S   K F C   S P U R
O T H E R   W A Y   S T Y
    E W E   A P A R T
A S I   N I T   P E E P S
T I C   E S E   S P A R E
A X E   W A R   S M E E
```

22

```
A R E   C O T   S W A Y
R A M   A I R   S T A T E
T W O   F L U   T A X E S
    T I E   T H E Y
A P I N   W H E E   S K I
S O O N E R O R L A T E R
H E N   N E R D   B A N K
    B E N D   P E P
B R O O M   A G O   L A W
E A R L Y   R A N   E Y E
D Y E D   E G G   R E D
```

23

```
  P E T S   F I R   A L L
  E X A M   A R E   S E A
  R I C E K R I S P I E S
    S O L E   S E E
B A T   L E G   T E L L S
I T E M   P A D   L O O K
T O D A Y   P U T   O U I
    Y E S   M A P S
C O C O A P E B B L E S
O N A   R U G   L E N T
W E T   S N O   E A S Y
```

24

```
B A A   T O Y   P L A N S
O I L   I D O   E A T U P
B R A   L O U I S I A N A
    B E E R   R O D
P R A Y S   S O S   I T O
R O M E   M A N   K N E W
O N A   C O W   T I D A L
    A H A   D I D I
W I S C O N S I N   A C T
A C H E S   A N T   N O R
G E E S E   Y E S   A N Y
```

25

```
LAW   ACT   TACO
ICE   PARK  AMAN
MEASURINGCUPS
BORE  DEER  SEE
 FEES SEA   EST
   PUT  SIP
PAT   SHE   NODS
ERR   HIPS  SITE
COOKIECUTTERS
AMMO  FORA  GAP
NAPS   TEN   OWN
```

26

```
DIED  FISH  MAP
IDEA  ONTO  USE
GOLDENSUN   SAW
   SAD  BOLT
GAB   TOW   REARS
ATOP  FAR   TRIO
SANTA RIB   DON
   FACT  POX
SKI   HONEYMOON
HER   EDEN  ACNE
EYE   SOWS  STAT
```

27

```
DIMS  MAT   AMMO
OVAL  ORA   PAUL
HYDE  AMS   EDGE
   MEAN  TEST
FRATS HEX   EAR
RUG   IREST ALE
ONA   AIR   RAPID
   ZINC  LALA
WAIT  HEE   ARTS
ANNE  EGG   STAN
STEM  ROO   TYPO
```

28

```
PIPE  LADY
IDOL  ACRE  TOP
SICK  INAN  EGO
AOK   GREW  NERD
 TELLS  STONES
   TIE   ANY
MISSED  CROWD
ARIA  ALOT  EAT
LIZ   OVER  MENU
ESE   NINE  ONCE
   ADDS  EYES
```

29

```
HAT   FOUR  SUM
ABS   LIFE  APP
SCHOOLOFFISH
  ITSY  ILL
CARTS SLY   PAT
INTO  SOL   SHOE
ADS   AMS   SCALE
  IDO   SCAN
HERDOFCATTLE
AGO   TEAR  OAR
DON   HERE  MDS
```

30

```
JAR   OLD   BELOW
AGE   TEA   LAURA
MOM   HAMBURGER
  OPEN  YEN
RIVER ITS   JET
OVEN  ACE   BETH
BED   TRY   PEACE
  SAM   HEEL
SLOPPYJOE   OIL
EERIE ALL   UNO
COATS YES   SAT
```

31

```
MAMA AIM SPAT
ARAB SCI IAGO
REDS LIL DREW
EAR SEEDS INN
  SITTER COST
   DRIP HALF
ASIN MINERS
DIP GOODS ACE
ISAY DAD SNOW
ALIE ONE ACRE
LENS RAN TEES
```

32

```
MOTH SUM SPA
EURO OFA HAD
TRANSFORMERS
   KIT TADA
DARES LIP DEM
ICED HEN REAR
PTA POT HOSTS
  CHAT CUB
 THELEGOMOVIE
EEL LOW TONS
ADD SOS SWAP
```

33

```
ABC SWAY ESPN
DYE LANE AQUA
DENTISTS RUNG
  TOP INA
GAIN BART RIP
ARM ARIES EVE
GEE CARD AMEN
  TIE ALI
EDEN CADILLAC
BURN USED EGO
BOSS PANS SOW
```

34

```
GAME WHIM ILL
AGED RATE TIE
LONGTIMENOSEE
  EAT MUD
JAW GEM SOLAR
ASIP RAP RACE
MINUS TAB BED
  RAN NUT
SHORTANDSWEET
HOW ASIA IAGO
EEL NAPS GROW
```

35

```
  SIDE ATMS
OFF AMEN CHAT
ALI SANG TUNA
TENTH SAW MIS
SAGA SEGA BAH
  ERIC EXIT
PAR SHED DATA
ELF HER OSCAR
CLOD MOAN KIM
ATOE EDGE SLY
NODS SEES
```

36

```
CAGES ZOO TOP
ALIVE APP AWE
RAVEN PER KEN
  ENDS NAME
SKI SOB HAPPY
OATH WED TREE
STABS DOS ITS
  ROAD CHAD
HOE LIP OCEAN
INS ACE RHINO
MET DEW TENTS
```

37

A	D	D		H	E	S		H	E	R	B
S	U	E		O	A	K		A	L	I	E
H	O	M	E	R	S	I	M	P	S	O	N
	A	N	N	E		A	P	E			
W	I	N	D	S		S	K	Y		C	U	B
O	D	D	S		D	U	E		C	A	P	E
N	O	S		T	E	N		P	U	R	S	E
		S	E	E		C	A	F	E		
P	E	T	E	R	G	R	I	F	F	I	N
E	V	E	N		A	I	R		U	S	A
N	E	W	S		B	B	S		L	A	G

38

U	H	U	H		H	U	S	H		D	E	W
S	I	T	E		A	S	I	A		E	M	O
A	P	A	R	T	M	E	N	T		J	I	M
	S	H	O	E					D	A	N	E
			E	D	I	T		O	V	E	N
C	O	N	D	O	M	I	N	I	U	M
T	A	P	E		T	A	C	O			
I	M	E	T				A	C	R	E
D	E	N		T	O	W	N	H	O	U	S	E
A	R	E		O	R	E	O		A	L	P	S
L	A	D		N	E	E	D		L	E	N	S

39

	N	U	N	S		A	B	S		O	F	F
	O	F	I	T		S	E	E		R	O	O
T	O	N	Y	T	H	E	T	I	G	E	R
		A	L	I			S	P	A		
N	O	R		E	L	S	A		O	N	A	N
O	B	E	Y		T	E	N		D	I	N	E
D	I	N	O		S	A	G	S		C	O	T
		E	G	G			R	O	D		
C	O	W	A	R	D	L	Y	L	I	O	N
A	W	E		A	R	E		A	C	N	E
B	E	D		B	Y	E		R	E	E	D

40

R	U	I	N		C	A	T	S		G	A	B
U	N	T	O		A	S	I	A		O	N	E
G	O	O	D	G	R	I	E	F		O	D	D
			S	A	P		S	E	N	D		
B	O	G		P	E	R		R	O	B	O	T
A	L	O	G		T	A	B		W	A	R	E
A	D	O	R	E		M	R	S		R	A	N
			D	R	A	W		I	O	U		
L	A	B		G	O	O	D	S	P	O	R	T
I	C	Y		L	O	N	G		O	R	E	O
T	E	E		E	L	S	E		N	E	X	T

ALSO AVAILABLE

ABOUT THE AUTHOR

TRIP PAYNE is a professional puzzle constructor and editor from Sherman Oaks, California. He made his first puzzles when he was in elementary school, had his first puzzle in a national magazine when he was in high school, and worked for a major puzzle magazine when he was in college. Aside from all the books in the *Crosswords for Kids* series, he has made kids' puzzles for such places as *Scholastic News*, *Games Junior*, and *TV Guide*. You can visit his website at tripleplaypuzzles.com and follow him on Twitter @PuzzleTrip.